CHRISTMAS CRACKERS (2)

Compiled by

Phil Mason

ISBN 0 948852 00 3

Published by
NORHEIMSUND BOOKS AND CARDS
1 Whitney Road
Burton Latimer
Kettering
Northants NN15 5SL

Have you a Sense of Humour?

This was the question we asked in 'Christian Crackers' (1).

We soon had the answer, for in a month the first edition had sold out.

Within six months over 7,000 copies had been sold with orders arriving from all over the world.

We received letters addressed to 'Christian Crackers', phone calls asking for 'Christian Crackers', cheques made payable to 'Christian Crackers', and many requests for more.

The result is 'Christian Crackers (2)', more humorous stories about church life that bring out chuckles in the most unexpected places.

Acknowledgements

We are most grateful to everyone who has contributed items. We received so many it has been impossible to include them all, but hopefully more will appear in 'Christian Crackers (3)'.

To the best of our knowledge permission has been sought to reproduce items that have previously appeared in other publications.

PHIL and MARY MASON

Parson Thoughts

Seen in a church magazine
If any readers have either a single bed or a man's bicycle to enable the vicar to get around his scattered parish Mr. Jones would be pleased to collect them.

The rector announced:
"After the blessing the bishop will leave and we shall sing 'Now thank we all our God' ".

The donkey failed to arrive for the Palm Sunday procession at St. Peter's church Chippenham. The procession was led by the Vicar, the Revd. Jeremy Bray.

Wiltshire Gazette

"Drink" said the Irish preacher "is the curse of the country. It makes ye quarrel with yer neighbours, it makes ye shoot at yer Landlord, and it makes ye miss him".

St. Matthew's magazine Upper Clapton

OVERHEARD IN THE VESTRY: "The congregation's a bit thin this morning" said the Vicar. "Did you tell them I was preaching?"
"No, Vicar, I didn't" replied the churchwarden. "But you know how things get out".

The Vicar moved to a new country Parish where the Post Office was the central point for village gossip. For some weeks he had the feeling that his parishioners were laughing at him behind his back. Finally he asked his Churchwarden what the source of this amusement was. The churchwarden told him that a postcard sent to the Vicar by a member of his former church had been read by the Postmistress, and she had told the others that it had said, "The new Vicar is very nice, and his sermons good, but he doesn't hold me the way that you used to".

Vicar to parishioner: "Did you like my sermon on 'The milk of human kindness'?"
Parishioner: "Yes, but I wish it had been condensed".

Some Baby

The minister had travelled from Birmingham to London to attend to the details of a new banner that was being made for his church. On his arrival he discovered that he had lost the piece of paper with the details on. He sent his wife a telegram asking her to send details by return. When the answer arrived at the Post Office the Postmistress almost fainted when she read:

"UNTO US A CHILD IS BORN. EIGHT FEET LONG.
THREE FEET WIDE. ASSORTED COLOURS".

A Blessing

What did the priest say to his ancient car?
May you rust in peace.

At a crowded church meeting the Vicar asked "Can you all hear me at the back?". A voice at the back said, "Yes, I can hear you perfectly well but I don't mind changing with somebody who can't".

For Better For Worse

"I hope you will be happy" said the Vicar to the newly married. "I don't see why not" said the bridegroom, "I came through the war alright". H.F.

The day after our wedding we were staying in Somerset on our honeymoon where we attended church. The service started earlier than we had been informed and as we entered the church 'with faces red at being late' the Vicar announced the hymn "My father for another night of quiet sleep and rest". M.V.

Misprint

The lady who typed the notices and hymn sheets in a Canadian Church sometimes hit the wrong key.

On one occasion when the hymn should have read

"be sure, he bids you" she had typed "be sure, he beds you". T.K.

The Prebysterian Church in Ireland brought out a new hymn book. In the first print a hymn for funerals was unfortunately included in the marriage section.

The Hymn was

"Go, happy soul, thy days are ended". R.R.

From Canada

One of the first weddings my husband conducted as a young curate was a farce. The bride, about eight months pregnant chewed gum all the way up the aisle, whilst the bridegroom and his mates were almost inebriated. My husband took a deep breath and said:

"Dearly beloved, we are gathered together IN SPITE OF GOD".

The organist nearly fell off his stool laughing. T.K.

An Anglican clergyman conducting a marriage service said "If either of you know any impediment, why ye may not be jawfully loined together in Matrimony ye do now confess it. J.R.

From the Notices

The minister announced that the sermon on Sunday would be shorter than usual — five minutes at the most. The choir then rendered the Anthem 'IT IS ENOUGH'.

Notice in a Train Window

RESERVED FOR BARE METHODISTS

'(It appears that Methodists from Bare were spending a day at the seaside long before topless bathing was allowed.)

From Yorkshire

The Trout Inn which lies between the village of Wansford and Driffield at the foot of the Yorkshire Wolds is a popular port of call for cyclists and ramblers. The elderly Vicar of Wansford asked the Innkeeper if he would display a notice giving details of the services at the village church. The Innkeeper gladly obliged and the notice read:

WE WILL BE GLAD TO SEE YOU AT ANY OF OUR SERVICES
CLOTHES DON'T MATTER   M.R.

Seen on a Church Notice Board

UNLIKE THE POST OFFICE WE HAVE TWO COLLECTIONS EVERY SUNDAY.

From the Mission Field

The Sacristan was so pleased to inform the congregation that their priest had recovered from his illness. He displayed the following notice.

GOD IS GOOD
THE VICAR IS BETTER

Church Times

True Stories

Taking the Mike

The Bishop had come to dedicate a new sophisticated public address system. Being unsure as to whether the microphone had been switched on or not he tapped it gently with seemingly no result. So, leaning very close to the microphone he said in a loud whisper which echoed around the church,

"THERE IS SOMETHING WRONG WITH THIS MICROPHONE".

The well trained and responsive congregation, well established in the latest A.S.B. service replied:

"AND ALSO WITH YOU".

D.G.

Holy Water

A Baptismal service was in progress at our local Baptist Church. During the course of his sermon the minister looked down at the water in the Baptistry and said, "There is nothing magical about this water. It is the same water that we shall use to make the coffee with later".

M.M.

The Last Word

The young curate didn't get on too well with his rather pompous vicar. In due course he was appointed to another church and for his last sermon in the parish he chose as his text:

"Tarry ye here with the ass while I go yonder".   F.H.

The same Vicar went on holiday to Jerusalem where, to the surprise of his flock, he met the lady of his choice. News of his forthcoming marriage soon reached the parish and the following Sunday the organist marked the event by playing the voluntary 'Pray for the peace of Jerusalem'.

F.H.

Lighten Our Darkness

On the Sunday after Christmas at St. Mark's Church Hamilton Terrace, London the lights failed just as Evensong was about to commence. Undaunted the curate and congregation found one or two candles and in the almost complete darkness of this large church proceeded with the service.

Meanwhile (unknown to the others) the Youth Club leader, an electrician by trade, had gone down to the Crypt to check fuses.

At the opening sentence of the third collect "LIGHTEN OUR DARKNESS WE BESEECH THEE O LORD" the lights came on again.

A.H.

Whilst in the Maternity ward of our local hospital awaiting the arrival of our baby the minister came to take a service and I chose a hymn I thought everyone would know: 'What a friend we have in Jesus'.

There was a good deal of chuckling amongst the expectant mothers as we sang:

'Are we weak and heavy-laden,

Cumbered with a load of care?'.   M.T.

A lady was very nervous about her appointment with the dentist. Before leaving home she sought courage by reading the text for the day from her calendar.

It was Psalm 81 verse 10

"OPEN THY MOUTH WIDE AND I WILL FILL IT".   M.P.

Poplar Saints

In the good old days the parishes from East London used to get the schoolchildren to church on Ascension Day and then take them off for an outing. The popular place for All Saints Poplar was Chessington Zoo. When 5 p.m. came there was a great gathering-up operation by Vicars, curates, and sisters on the large green. A loud voice called across the green to our lot boarding the coach, "Are you Holy Innocents?". And the shout went back "No, we're all SAINTS".   J.P.

A friend of mine used to help an undertaker when required. One frosty morning a lady coming out of the Crematorium slipped on the ice. An onlooker remarked "You'd think they would sprinkle a few ashes around here wouldn't you?".   M.D.

Asked how many people worked in the Vatican, Pope John XXIII replied, "Oh about half".

From Scotland

The story goes that some delegates to a church conference in Scotland set off between sessions to explore the countryside. Presently they came to a stream spanned by a rickety bridge and started to cross, ignoring the warning to keep off.

A local inhabitant ran after them in protest. Not understanding his concern one of the visitors said "It's alright, we are Anglicans from the Conference".

"I'm no caring about that" was the reply, "but if ye dinna get off the bridge ye'll all be Baptists".   R.P.

Spotted on a Church Notice Board

When you were born, your mother brought you here,
When you were married, your partner brought you here,
When you die your friends will bring you here,
Why not try coming on your own sometimes?   R.P.

There were two Sunday fishermen who heard bells ringing in the distance. One said contritely: "You know, Sam, we really ought to be in church". Sam rebaited his hook and answered: "Well, I couldn't go anyway, my wife is sick".   R.P.

An Anglican Archbishop and a Roman Catholic Archbishop both died. When they reached the pearly gates Peter ushered them into a waiting room. After they had been kicking their heels for an hour or so a pretty girl arrived and was ushered straight in. At this their Graces protested asking why such a youngster should get preferential treatment over men of their standing. St. Peter looked at them a moment and said: "That young girl has just crashed in her sports car which she learned to drive a year ago. In that short year she has put the fear of God into more people than your Graces have in the whole of your lives".   R.P.

From Cornwall

During prayers at the Primitive Methodist Chapel in St. Ives one of the members cried out in fervour:

"Come down through the roof Lord, and we'll pay the expenses".

The answer came immediately, when a piece of the ceiling fell with a loud crash into the chapel.   R.R.

From a Baptist News Sheet

The Deacons Meeting on Thursday will be gin with prayer.

From Warwickshire

The Wedding music chosen by two young vegetarians included the voluntary 'Sheep may safely graze'.   *The Daily Telegraph*

No Monkeying About

A clergyman who stuttered rather badly, and who spent many years abroad as a Missionary was asked what had sustained him most over the years. "Oh, that's easy," he said, "My Wife, she has b-b-been a great b-big b-boon to me".

To Obey

There was a queue of men standing at the Pearly Gates waiting to enter. A sign overhead read "FOR MEN WHO HAVE BEEN DOMINATED BY THEIR WIVES". The queue extended as far as the eye could see. Close by there was another sign which said "FOR MEN WHO HAVE NEVER BEEN DOMINATED BY THEIR WIVES". Just one man was standing underneath it. St. Peter came over to him and asked, "Why are you standing here?". "I don't really know" he replied, "except my wife told me to".

From Cornwall

To oblige a customer who wanted the *'Church Times'* the newsagent searched through a pile of papers only to report, "I'm sorry, it hasn't come in yet. Several other comics are also late".

From The Irish Bulletin

There will be a procession next Sunday afternoon in the grounds of the monastery. If it should rain in the afternoon the procession will take place on Sunday morning.

Seen in a Connecticut Church Bulletin

Tuesday at 4 p.m. there will be an Ice Cream Social. All ladies giving milk please come early.

From the Mouths of Babes

A child on the way home from school decided to call in the church and have a look around. When he arrived home he told his Grandmother he had been in God's house. "Oh" said Grandma: "And did you see God?". "No" replied the little boy, "but I saw his wife scrubbing the floor".   M.E.

Said a little boy to his vicar:
"I don't pray every night because there are some nights when I don't need anything".

Endeavouring to impress the children with joyous exultation of Hallelujah, the Sunday School teacher said,
"What word do church members shout with joy?".
"Bingo" replied one youngster.

Nun Other

Two little boys had been having a very serious discussion, when one of them went up to the Sister who worked in the parish and said, "you're not one of them things that goes into the fields to scare the birds are you?"   S.A.

A little boy once wrote in his essay on 'Lying',
"A lie is an abomination unto the Lord but a very present help in trouble".

Finally

A young curate was visiting an elderly man on his 99th birthday to interview him about his long life. The interview over, the curate said "I hope to see you again on your 100th birthday". The old gentleman carefully looked him over and said, "I can't see any reason why you shouldn't, young man, you look healthy enough to me".

Grave Situations

Seen on a gravestone

Here lies a woman, no man can deny it,
She dies in peace although she lived unquiet,
Her husband prays that if this way you walk,
You would tread softly, if she awake she'll talk.

Gravestone Rhymes from Dr. David Owen:

Here lies Solomon Peas
Under the trees and sod
But peas is not here —
Only the pod
Peas shelled out and is gone to God.

Here lies the body of Mary Jones
Who died of eating cherry stones
Her name was Smith, it was not Jones
But Jones was put to rhyme with stones.

Direct Hit

The church members were meeting to discuss raising money to repair the roof. A wealthy member stood up and said he would donate £5. As he sat down a bit of ceiling fell on his head. He rose again and said he would make it £50. Another member was heard to say "Hit him again Lord".

From Liverpool

Bishop David Sheppard, former England cricketer, shares the following true story about his wife Grace, who is a Governor of a comprehensive school. On one occasion when the governors were interviewing for the appointment of Deputy Head the chairman of the governors introduced her with the words:
"This is Mrs. Bishop, the wife of the famous footballer".

From Scotland
David Steel has sent the following story

"At the annual church bazaar, our family gave a siamese kitten for a "guess the name" competition. Being black and white it was called "Whisky". When the winner was announced a deaf lady at the back of the hall said "disgraceful, Mrs. MacFarlane winning whiskey at a church event".

From Buckinghamshire
Roy Castle shares the following story

To commemorate the Feast of St. Francis the children brought their pets to church. Hamsters, Gerbils, Rabbits, etc. There was even a Parrot parading the pulpit. As the vicar settled everyone ready for prayer a pony was ridden rather noisily up the marble aisle. Stopping nose to nose with the vicar the young equestrian fought to turn the pony round. The manoeuvre was finally accomplished as we reached the part when we all say: "We have left undone those things which we ought to have done". Then as we reached the words "And we HAVE done those things which we ought NOT to have done", the pony DID.

When Antonia was six years old she was informed one Sunday that we were going to church. "Why?" she asked. "To learn about God" replied mother. Antonia frowned and complained "But we DO God at school".

Roy Castle

A Bishop speaking about the 'Water of Life' asked the younger members of the congregation where their drinking water came from. A little boy jumped up and quickly said
    "From the Lord my Pump".

When on holiday one year my brother and I attended the local church. On the way my brother had a fall which delayed us somewhat. We entered as the congregation were singing the first hymn:
    'Courage, brother, do not stumble'.

W.M.C.

Our choir sometimes visits hospitals etc. to give concerts. At one Old People's Home the organist announced that she would play *'Handel's Largo'.* An old lady sitting close by in a wheelchair said in a loud voice "Oh, I love a drop of lager".

A Cranford housewife was talking to an American visitor about the difficulty in getting domestic help. She added how lucky she was to have a daily help.
    "My" said the American, "Is that something religious?".

A vicar looked out of his window and saw an old tramp on his knees eating the grass on the front lawn. "My good man" he cried, "Whatever are you doing there?" "Well sir", the tramp replied, "I'm so hungry that I'm eating the grass".
    "Then go into the back garden" said the vicar. "You'll find it longer round there".

OTHER NORHEIMSUND PUBLICATIONS

include: —

CHRISTIAN CRACKERS —

the original booklet in this series which sold 7,000 copies
in six months.

FAITH SHARING SERIES

BRIDGES OF LOVE
MORE BRIDGES OF LOVE
BUILDING BRIDGES OF LOVE

MINI GIFT BOOKLETS

TOGETHER IN LOVE (Wedding booklet)
WITH SYMPATHY, LOVE AND PRAYERS (for the bereaved)
JOINING THE FAMILY (for those being baptised)
CHRISTMAS WISHES
CHRISTMAS GREETINGS
THINKING OF YOU

ALSO: —

WELCOME TO LONDON'S CHURCHES —

a succinct guide to ten central London Churches with details
of services, how to get there, etc.